C000294834

* Please do not remove *

Walks on Tiree, Coll, Colonsay and a taste of Mull

Walks on Tiree, Coll, Colonsay and a taste of Mull

by

Mary Welsh

Maps and Illustrations by Christine Isherwood

Westmorland Gazette, Kendal, Cumbria

First published 1996

ISBN 0 902272 98 5

© Westmorland Gazette, 1996

Published by
Westmorland Gazette
22 Stricklandgate, Kendal, Cumbria

Printed by
Miller Turner Printers Limited
The Sidings, Beezon Fields, Kendal, Cumbria

Foreword

The earth unto the Lord belongs
And all that it contains
Except Western isles and piers
For they are Caledonian MacBrayne's

The lovely islands Mary Welsh writes about in her delightful book are among the ones referred to in the old poem and as MacBrayne's Area Manager I visit them frequently and know them well. Always I carry a pair of walking shoes in my car and whenever I get the chance, between ferries or at the end of the day, in the gloaming I'm off across the machair, along some deserted beach or into the hills.

I can remember the walks detailed in this book and hope that readers will enjoy walking in the islands as much as I do.

William Kindness
Area Manager
Western Isles (South)
Caledonian MacBrayne

Acknowledgments

It is a great pleasure to walk on the lovely islands of Tiree, Coll, Colonsay and Mull. I received much help in producing this book and my grateful thanks go to my friend Maureen Fleming for her help in researching and checking the walks; to Christine Isherwood, who has illustrated them so delightfully, encouraging walkers to seek out the sights for themselves; to Caledonian MacBrayne for their kindly support; to the Oban Tourist Board, who gave me so much friendly help and advice; to Jean Cowling for her careful copy-editing; and to my husband Tom for his constant support.

Author's Note

Please remember on all these walks:

Wear suitable clothes and take adequate waterproofs.

Walk in strong footwear; walking boots are advisable.

Carry the relevant map and know how to use it.

Take extra food and drink as emergency rations.

Carry a whistle; remember six long blasts repeated at one minute intervals is the distress signal.

Do not walk alone, and tell someone where you are going.

If mist descends, return.

Close all gates. Respect walls and fences.

On these walks there are many sheep and many sheer cliffs over which they may fall if chased; keep all dogs under close control.

Readers are advised that while the author has taken every effort to ensure the accuracy of this guidebook, changes can occur after publication. You should check locally on transport, accommodation, etc. The publisher would welcome notes of any changes. Neither the publisher nor the author can accept responsibility for errors, omissions or any loss or injury.

Location Map

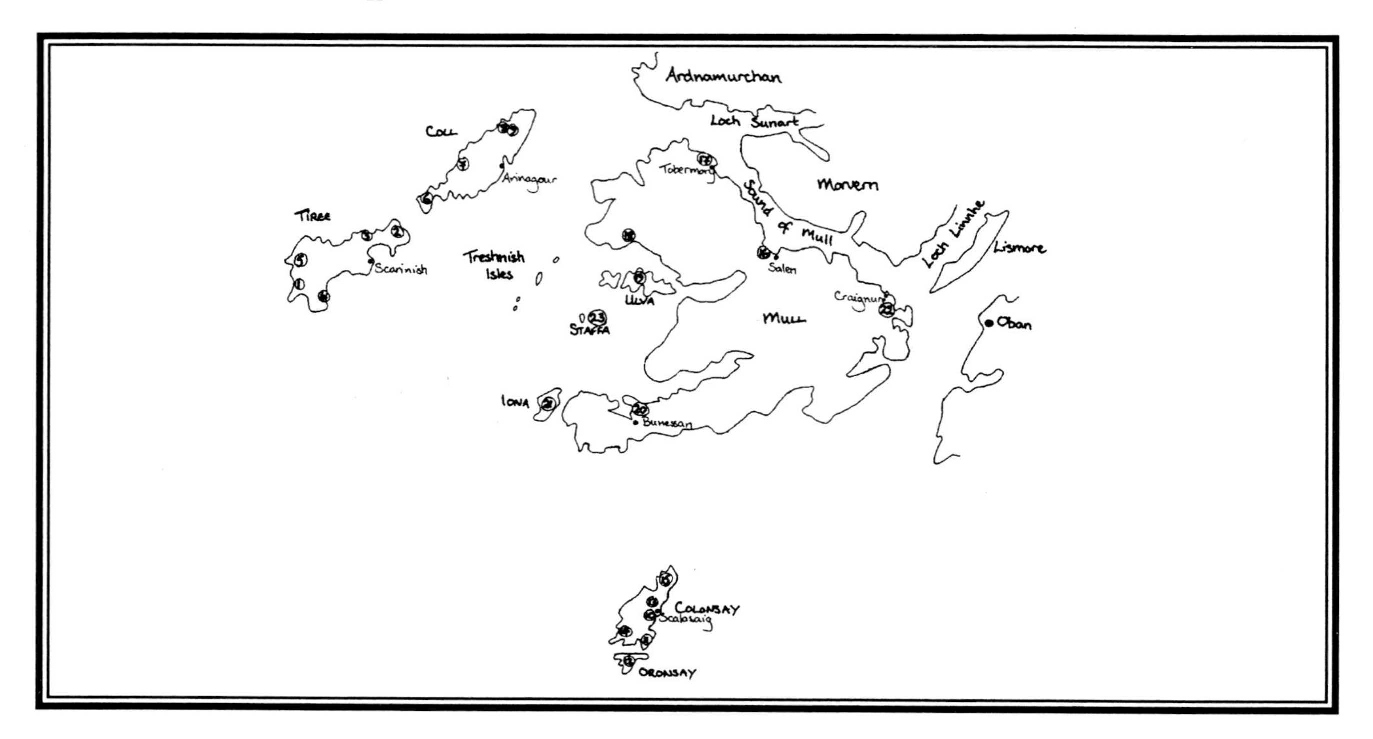

Contents

Walk Number		Miles	Page Number
1	Circular Walk around Kenavara, Tiree	5	11
2	Circular Walk from Salum, Tiree	8	15
3	Circular Walk from Vaul, Tiree	6	19
4	Linear Walk from Hynish, Tiree	2	23
5	Circular Walk to Beinn Hough, Tiree	4 ½	26
6	Circular Walk around the West Coast of Coll	8 ½	29
7	Circular Walk from Totronald, Coll	5 ½	33
8	Circular Walk around Cornaigbeg, North-East Coll	2 ½	36
9	Linear Walk to Loch Fada, Coll	3 ½	39
10	Circular Walk from the Pier, Colonsay	1	41
11	Circular Walk below Beinn Eibhne, Colonsay	3 ½	43
12	Linear Walk to the Isle of Oronsay	5	45
13	Circular Walk from the Pier across Colonsay's Rocky Spine	5	48
14	Circular Walk to Ardskenish, Colonsay	6½-7	51
15	Linear Walk from Kiloran Bay to Balnahard Bay, Colonsay	6	54
16	Circular Walk from Salen, Mull	4 ½	57
17	Circular Walk from Tobermory, Mull	2 ½	60
18	Circular Walk overlooking Loch Tuath, Mull	9	63
19	Walk on Ulva, close to the West Coast of Mull	10	67
20	Circular Walk from Ardtun, Mull	4	71
21	Circular Walk on the Isle of Iona	7½	74
22	Circular Walk from Craignure, Mull	2	79
23	Walk on the Isle of Staffa	2	81

Tiree

Tiree is the furthest west of the islands that make up the Inner Hebrides. The bedrock is gneiss, but the creamiest of shell sand covers nearly the whole island. Crofthouses are to be found scattered throughout and an air of bustle, contentment and friendliness prevails.

The island is very flat, but it has three hills, none higher than 460 feet. It is 12 miles long and varies in width from one to six miles. There are few trees.

Caledonian MacBrayne operates a passenger and vehicle ferry from Oban, which takes five hours if it calls first at Tobermory and Coll. You arrive at Scarinish on the south-east side of the island. Inland stretch single-track metalled roads, with passing places marked with black and white posts. They carry very little traffic and are a pleasure to walk. Indeed, nearly all of Tiree is grand for walking; there are few places you cannot go. Please remember as you walk to shut all gates.

There is hotel, guest-house, self-catering and bed-and-breakfast accommodation.

Coll

Coll is an island of bare rock and heather, green pastures and sand dunes. It is edged with glorious silver-sand bays that are hemmed by cliffs, crags and whale-backs of gneiss. A wonderful view is obtained from its highest hill, Beinn Hogh (339 feet). The island is 12 miles long and three to four miles wide.

Most of the small population live in the village of Arinagour at the head of Loch Eatharna. Caledonian MacBrayne vehicle and passenger ferries link Arinagour with Oban, via Tobermory, several times a week. They take just over three hours to complete the journey.

The pier, constructed in 1969, provides good access to the

boats and there is a short walk along the road to the village. The roads are narrow but good and are a delight to walk.

The island provides hotel, guest-house, self-catering and bed-and-breakfast accommodation.

Colonsay

Colonsay is an island of rocky outcrops of Torridon sandstone containing lime. The soil supports heather, bog myrtle and deer grass. Scattered over the island are cultivated areas where hay and silage are grown and cattle graze. The western coast is riven and wild with many delectable sheltered golden sandy bays. One great stretch at the southern end, The Strand, gives access to the delightful island of Oronsay. Colonsay is three miles wide and eight miles long - ten miles in length if you include Oronsay.

A metalled road leads from the pier at Scalasaig and completes a circle through this prosperous-looking island. From it, by driving and then walking, you can reach all the lovely hidden gems that Colonsay has to offer.

Colonsay House, with its famous collection of trees and a magnificent variety of rhododendrons, lies towards the northern end of the island. Its mature woodland shelters it from the westerly gales.

Caledonian MacBrayne's passenger and vehicle ferry from Oban takes two-and-a-half hours and anchors at the excellent pier at Scalasaig. There is a once-a-week service from Kennacraig on Kintyre (three-and-a-half hours) or Port Askaig on Islay (one hour). Hotel, guest-house, self-catering and bed-and-breakfast accommodation is offered on the island.

Mull

Mull lies in the Firth of Lorne, separated by the Sound of Mull from Morvern on the mainland. It is up to 20 miles in width in places, and approximately 25 miles long.

It is a big island compared to Tiree, Coll and Colonsay, and has high hills and long, lonely glens. The vegetation is more grass than heather, and conifer plantations and some deciduous woodland of birch, ash and oak cover its slopes. Ben More, a Munro, and its surrounding hills, dominate the scenery of the island and can be seen from other islands and the mainland.

The island has basalt cliffs, which are at their most dramatic at Ardmeanach peninsula, with its great terraced lava flows. Delightful sandy bays encircled by pink granite cliffs, and numerous waterfalls can also be found.

It is reached from Oban by Caledonian MacBrayne passenger and vehicle ferry, which berths at Craignure. From this anchorage, it is but a short distance, south, to the castles of Duart and Torosay, both open to the public and both with magnificent gardens. The ruined Aros Castle lies in the opposite direction, beyond Salen.

The Caledonian MacBrayne ferry also calls at Tobermory but only to allow passengers to embark and disembark. ; ferries run from Lochaline, Morvern and Kilchoan, Ardnamurchan. It is helpful to have a car when visiting this lovely island, but bicycles can be hired, and a convenient bus service links the main centres of population. There are hotels, guest houses, self-catering and bed-and-breakfast accommodation, but these should be booked in advance. Camping is possible, but seek permission of the landowner.

For more information about the islands, contact West Highlands and Islands Tourist Board, Oban - telephone 01631 63122; and, Caledonian MacBrayne, Oban - telephone 01631 66688.

1. A Circular Walk around Kenavara, Tiree

Information	
Distance:	5 miles one way
Time:	3 hours
Map:	Pathfinder 314, NL 94/NM 04 Tiree reference 945426 (parking)
Terrain:	Generally easy walking. Steep climb at start of ascent. Take care on the cliffs. Shut all gates and close securely.

This walk explores Kenavara (Ceann a' Mhara), a rugged, precipitous and deeply riven pink gneiss headland some 300 feet in height, which lies to the south west of Tiree. After you drive through the island and cross the totally flat area known as The Reef, Kenavara presents a great surprise.

Kenavara (Ceann a' Mhara)

Park on the grassy verge where the B8065 turns sharply right towards Sandaig. Pass through a gate to a good cart-track and stride ahead over the sandy way. Look out for golden plovers running over the turf. Follow the route through the pale dunes to pass through two more gates. Stroll on

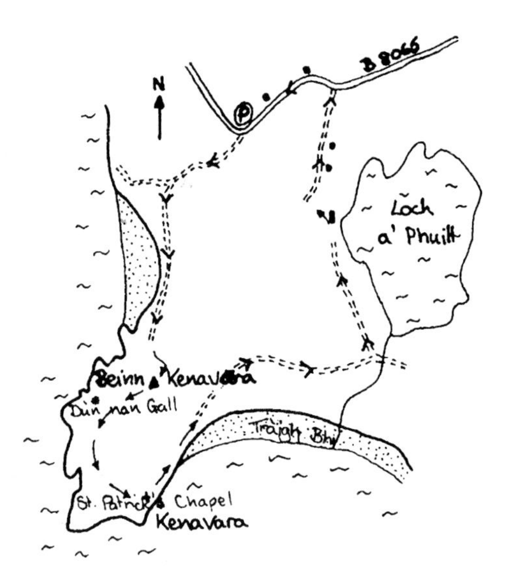

towards the next fence and, just before it, bear left to walk the sward.

Beyond the next gate, follow the track through the dunes, where several hares disport. After two more gates, turn left and begin the steep climb up the north side of Kenavara, keeping the fence to your left. (It would be pleasant to continue and avoid this climb but a huge sheer-sided inlet prevents your progress round the headland.)

Once at the ridge, strike right, steadily climbing to the summit, Mullach Mór, on which stands a small cairn. Wander around this glorious top. Enjoy the wild flowers and the catkin-laden dwarf willow. Look out to sea, where Skerryvore Lighthouse stands like a tall thin pencil. It was designed by Alan Stevenson and was largely built of red granite from Ross of Mull. Overhead fulmars and kittiwakes fly to their nests on the many ledges of the cliffs. These are occasionally disturbed by a pair of ravens, and the deep ravines echo their indignant calls. Look inland to see the large shallow sandy Loch a' Phuill and, to its south, the magnificent curve of the seashore, Tràigh Bhi. Whatever the weather, the gleaming sand brightens the day.

As you leave the top, look for the old wall running down to the shoulder and then up again towards the southerly headland. Just as you begin to climb, look seaward along a long rocky sheer-sided promontory. Close to its natural cairn, an upstanding sturdy tussock of grass created by erosion, is the site of a dun, one of several thought to have been constructed on Kenavara.

Continue around the delightful headland. Here, more fulmars nest among dark pink campion, scurvy grass and primrose. Lower down on some dark, dank ledges, shags sit on their untidy nests. Follow the fence round and then steadily drop down, over colourful lousewort, towards the beach. Here stand the remains of St Patrick's Chapel. Then follow the narrow path to the start of Tràigh Bhi. Notice the many low stone walls, enclosing oblong areas, once used for drying kelp. Tiree has no peat, and the islanders relied on a thriving kelp industry to provide the money to buy peat from other islands.

Nesting fulmar with primroses and campion

When you can bear to leave the lovely bay, take a grassy track, with wheel marks, that leads away from the western end of the sands. Follow this across the machair, keeping well above the majority of high dunes. This track comes to the side of the narrow river that flows out of the loch, seen from the top of Kenavara.

Do not cross the cattle grid and bridge over the river, but turn left instead to follow a similar grassy track that runs parallel with the west shore of the loch. This is a wonderful place for bird watching. Look for whooper swans, redshanks and dunlin. Overhead wheel innumerable green plover.

Pass a derelict farm and, at the fence, turn left. Take a gate on your right that gives access to a re-inforced gated track. Follow this track all the way to the road. Turn left and walk the quiet way to rejoin your car. Listen as you go for the 'creek-creek' of the corncrake.

2. A Circular Walk from Salum, Tiree

Information

Distance:	8 miles
Time:	4-5 hours
Map:	Pathfinder 314, NL 94/NM 04 Tiree, reference 064478 (parking)
Terrain:	Generally easy.

This is a delightful walk around the north-eastern coast of Tiree. It follows tracks and pathless ways along the rocky coastline, and takes you over glorious shell-sand bays.

Park on the B8069, just after the road leaves Tràigh Mhór and heads inland. Walk on to take the next left turn, signposted to Salum. In pastures beside the road, redshanks feed. At the eastern end of Salum Bay. opposite the last farm on the road, cross left to the shore. Here a tumble of boulders is all that remains of a massive causeway to An Dùnan, a little fort on an isolated grass-covered rock. At high tide, water surrounds it.

Common seals on skerry

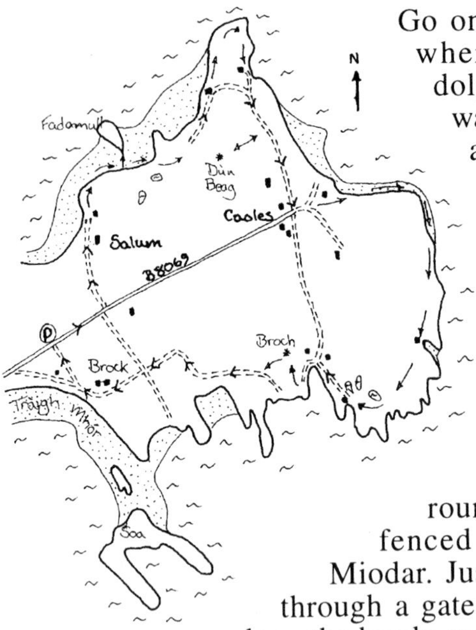

Go on around the shoreline, where you might see dolphins disporting in the water and seals basking on a skerry. Half a mile from the dun look for the green Fadamull, once a tidal island, now connected to the shore by a ridge of boulders. See the remains of the ancient causeway that once provided the link.

Follow the shore round to join a walled and fenced track leading towards Miodar. Just before the farm, pass through a gate on the left, to continue along the lovely sandy shore. Press on along the pleasant machair, keeping to the outside of a low stone wall. Look for hares racing off across the pastures. At the northernmost tip, where a mass of large boulders has been deposited by the tides, look across Gunna Sound to the island of Gunna and beyond to Coll.

As you round the point, MacNeill's Port lies to your left. Southwards you can see the Treshnish Isles, with the island named The Dutchman's Cap standing bold. Beyond lies Mull.

At the dwelling of Urvaig, a track continues ahead. On reaching the first cattle grid, walk right beside the fence on your left to a large green mound that lies up against a dyke. This is Dùn Beag. Return to the road and walk on to pass a red telephone box. After the next fence, bear left across the sandy turf to a stile over a fence. Then drop down the shallow cliffs to walk glorious sands beside turquoise water.

Leave the pleasing bay by a typical Tiree house built of local stone, the mortar being whitened and the stones left uncovered. Stroll on to pass a wooden house with shutters, where daffodils flower in profusion among the boulders of the low cliffs. Keep up on the cliffs, striding over dwarf willow and heather, to pass a cottage with a black felted roof at the head of Port Bàn.

A sheep trod continues. Follow this and keep to the rocky outcrops, so avoiding marshy troughs, to round the headland. Pass through a gap in a derelict wall and head for the roof tops and hydro-poles of Millton. Then stride a large shingle ridge to straddle a fence. Join a track by a renovated house, where an old blackhouse with five-feet thick walls has been incorporated into a pleasing dwelling. Follow the track through Millton, where you will see most of the few trees that grow on Tiree.

At a T-junction of tracks, bear left to walk past a small harbour used for lobster fishing. Pass through the gate and turn right to climb to the summit of the little hill (100 feet). Here stands a broch, Dùn Mòr a' Chaolais. Little remains of the circular dry-stone fortified dwelling, many of its stones having been used to construct a nearby wall. Next to the broch stands a fenced and covered reservoir. Pause on the hill to enjoy a spectacular view towards the mountains of Mull and the mainland, and over Coll to Rùm and the Cuillin of Skye.

Black house settlement, Broch

Descend towards the sea over mountain everlasting, a little white flower with pink tips and green leaves edged with white. Join a causeway track that bears right to run above dampish ground. Pass through a gate to walk a wide-fenced track, initially wet, but soon ditched on either side, where grow milkmaids, irises and kingcups.

Cross a narrow road and continue on. Bear right towards the huge curving sandy bay, Tràigh Mhór, to pass the small settlement of Broch. Here a dozen or more blackhouses have been pleasingly restored, with felted roof replacing thatch and many characteristic features retained.

Walk across the links over a grassy track and, as you near a red-roofed bungalow, take the right branch to rejoin your car.

3. A Circular Walk from Vaul, Tiree

Information	
Distance:	6 miles
Time:	3 hours
Map:	Pathfinder 314, NL 94/NM 04 Tiree, reference 051473 (parking)
Terrain:	Easy walking. Could be wet in places.

There is something of interest around each corner of this delightful walk. It takes you along a part of the glorious coast of Tiree, visits two duns, continues to a magic stone, and returns you first beside several lochs and then back along more silvery sands.

Park on the grassy sward just before the post box and the turn for the township of Vaul. Walk the narrow road towards Vaul, continuing beside the golf course, where sheep graze. Look out over the water to see the Cuillin of Skye peeping through the gap in the mountains of Rùm. To the right, with its distinctive cliffs, lies Eigg. To the left of Rùm you can just discern the Uists.

Where the road swings left, continue ahead along the shore and onto the shallow cliffs, from where you can see seals, eiders and shelduck. Continue round Vaul Bay to climb a steep-sided grassy hill, Dùn Beag, an Iron-Age fort, once impregnable from the sea. From the top you can see the island of Barra.

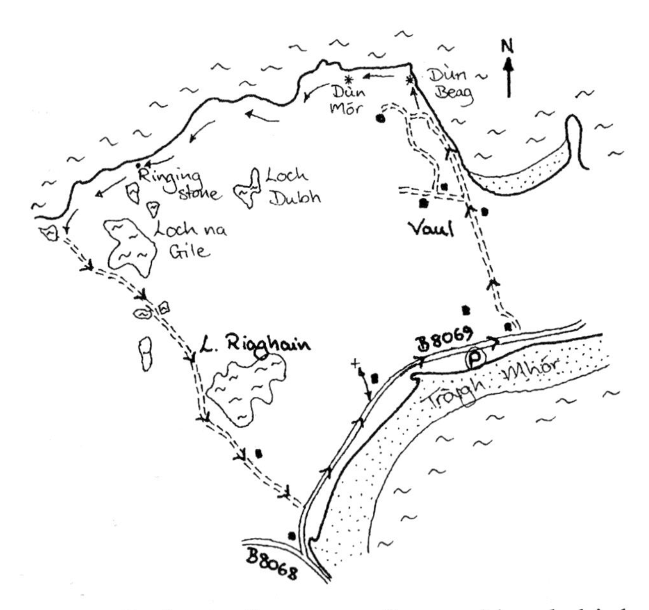

Go on to climb a stile over a fence. Ahead, high on its grassy hill, stands Dùn Mór Vaul, Tiree's most splendid broch. Climb into the circular dry-stone base of the one-time tower, which would have been a fortified home. Look for the steps and gallery. Outside you can trace a perimeter wall, perhaps where the cattle were coralled, or the family lived, moving into the tower in times of trouble. Sit in the flower-bedecked walled enclosure and ponder on the lives of these early occupants.

Return down the little path and walk on through vast outcrops of gneiss. Here, lousewort and butterwort grow, reminding you that it can be wet underfoot. Pass a delightful pool on your right, Loch an Fhaing, where a heron feeds and redshanks call. Look up on the highest outcrop for a pair of ravens, which grumble at any bird that comes too near.

At the fence, cross by an excellent stile to walk round a sandy bay. Overhead fly several honking greylag geese and these are sent away by one of the ravens. Continue on along the headland of gneiss, taking care as you round several sheer-sided ravines that pierce the way.

Follow a narrow path over a grassy sward and then pass, on the left, a wet area with small pools. Here, there are more geese, duck, eider, whimbrel, dunlin, ringed plovers and gulls. Then, as Loch Dubh a' Gharraidh Fàil comes into view, look to see a strange large grey formless boulder. This is the Ringing Stone, believed to be an erratic, a stone deposited by a glacier far from its origin - in this case Rùm. It stands on a plinth of rock and has many neat cup-shaped hollows in it. Strike the great boulder with a pebble and hear it ring. Legend says that if the rock is shattered, Tiree will be overwhelmed by the sea.

The Ringing Stone (Clach a' Choire)

Press on along the shore, which is littered with innumerable shells. Continue ahead until you come to a fence. Here, a track, a slightly raised causeway built to bring out the kelp collected on the shore, swings left, inland. It is a joy to walk and brings you close to Loch na Gile, a place for some bird watching. Head on through a very wet area where you appreciate the sturdy track, and then pass between two smaller

Red-breasted mergansers

lochs. Go through a gate (remember to close it) and walk to the right of Loch Riaghain, where whooper swans nest and a pair of mergansers swim.

Stroll on to join the narrow road at Gott Farm House. Stride on to the B8069, where you turn left and walk to Lodge Hotel. Turn left before it, to visit two ancient chapels constructed of stone and picturesquely covered in golden lichen. It is believed that the chapel within the burial ground dates from the 14th century. Spend time looking at the gravestones, some of which are very old. The little ruined chapel behind, standing alone on a hillock, is thought to be even older.

Return to the huge curving sands of Tràigh Mhór and continue to rejoin your car.

4. A Linear Walk from Hynish, Tiree

Information

Distance:	2 miles
Time:	An afternoon
Map:	Pathfinder 314, NL 94/NM 04 Tiree, reference 985393 (parking)
Terrain:	Easy walking except for the marshy area.

The cliffs on the sea side are sheer and, on the climb to the dun, children should be accompanied.

Hynish lies at the end of the B8066, on the south-west tip of Tiree, and a visit to the Signalling Tower Museum is a must. Its displays graphically show the great endeavour and endurance shown in the building of Skerryvore Lighthouse, 12 miles offshore on a dangerous reef. Afterwards, round off your visit to this end of the island with a gentle walk, wet in parts, to a hidden bay. Some will enjoy the climb to Dùn na Cleite and the magnificent views obtained from it.

Signalling Tower, Hynish

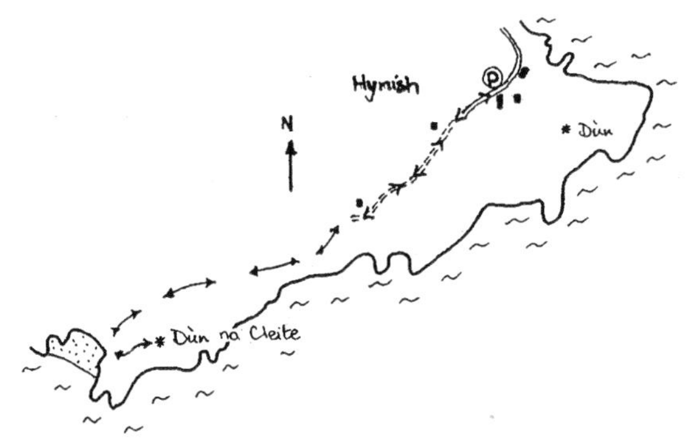

Park by the wall of the Signalling Tower Museum at Hynish. The key can be obtained from the middle cottage in a row of dwellings beside the tower.

So many ships and lives were lost on the isolated reef that Alan Stevenson, a member of the famous family of lighthouse builders, was asked to design and build the Skerryvore. It took five years to construct the 180-feet high lighthouse. The first support tower, from which the builders worked, was washed away and another had to be constructed. The pier at Hynish was built to handle the enormous quantity of material needed. The rocks, from Tiree and from the Ross of Mull, were cut and dressed onshore and then taken to the reef. This work was so well done that every huge block dovetailed exactly. The displays in the museum dramatically reveal the arduous nature of the job and point out that, throughout the five years of construction, no life was lost through accident.

The Signalling Tower was built as a shore-base and for communication, by flag signals, with the workers on the reef. The flat-roofed cottages housed the first lighthouse keepers and their families. Skerryvore, seen as a pencil-slim tower through binoculars in the museum, started beaming its light in 1844 and continued without ceasing until 1954, when a serious fire devastated it. It took nearly a year to restore.

It was from Hynish harbour that many emigrants from Tiree set sail for Canada in the middle of the 19th century. While in Hynish, visit the pier, look for the dock, the outlet from the reservoir for flushing out the dock, and the tenement with its

Osprey

grand stairway built for seamen.

To reach Happy Valley, as the hidden hollow is known, continue from the tower to the end of the road. Stride along the track to pass through a series of gates (please close). Go on. Negotiate the wet area to reach the long grassy valley, which is flanked by towering gneiss. The lonely vale slopes gently towards the sea. Beyond a huge wall of pebbles lies a delightful sandy bay.

Dùn na Cleite stands high on the left. Walk round the lower part of the hill; then an easy way to ascend is seen. The remains of two small walls, almost obscured by sand and vegetation, are all that is visible of the fort. Enjoy the magnificent view of Skerryvore Lighthouse standing proud on the horizon; erecting the dun must have been almost as arduous for Iron-Age builders as constructing the lighthouse was for the 19th-century workmen. From here you might also see an osprey being chased away by angry gulls and green plovers.

5. A Circular Walk to Beinn Hough, Tiree

Information

Distance:	4½ miles
Time:	2-3 hours
Map:	Pathfinder 314, NL 94/NM 04 Tiree, reference 940437 (parking)
Terrain:	Easy walking. Stout shoes or boots needed.

Look for the old mill if you drive through Cornaig. It still has its water wheel, which was fed by a leat from Loch Bhasapol behind.

For a wonderful panorama of the whole of the island, climb one of Tiree's three hills. This walk ascends Beinn Hough (388 feet) and then returns along three large magnificent sandy bays.

Park on the turf at Sandaig, reached from Heylipol by the B8065. Before setting off, visit the fascinating Sandaig Museum, where part of a terrace of thatched buildings, including houses, byres and barns, has been restored. Inside a dwelling house you can see the type of furniture used and the layout of the rooms.

Proceed north along the narrow road and continue for just over half a mile to two gates on the left, opposite a house named Kildunan. Pass through the second gate and head up beside the fence and then towards the left for a few yards to see the ancient chapel of St Kenneth, a friend of St Columba. The roofless ruin lies in the sand dunes, each stone heavily

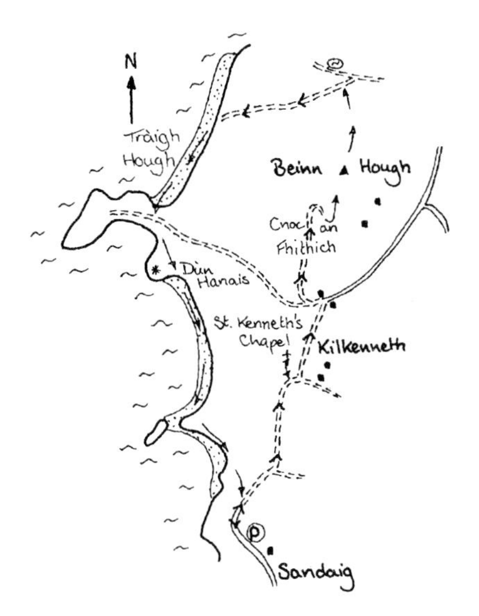

encrusted with golden lichen. Early in this century a small bronze bell was found in the remains.

Return to the gate and continue along the road to cross the cattle grid. Bear left along the road that climbs round the seaward side of Cnoc an Fhithich, where there are two tall masts. As you climb you can see Skerryvore Lighthouse, Barra and the Uists.

From the road up the hill, look left down a sloping sward, where a mass of deep purple marsh orchids flowers. Below, on wide grassy links, cattle graze about Loch Earblaig. At the first mast Loch a' Phuill and Kenavara come into view.

Bear left to climb to the next mast on the hill and then go along the airy way, with the sea to the left. Jura and Islay lie on the horizon. Drop down, with care, to a grassy glen and then ascend to the triangulation point on Beinn Hough. Pause here and enjoy the island spread out before you, flat, green, with deep blue lochs and golden curving bays. From this high point you can see the many cattle and sheep, and crofters ploughing and rolling their land.

Descend by some concrete steps, which are edged with concrete posts, and, when these swing right, go on, climbing down steadily to the sandy links. Look for more marsh orchids on the way. Pass through a gate in the fence, walk over to join the track, and bear left. Follow the reinforced way to Tràigh Hough and stroll the sands to the end. Look for white

Northern marsh orchid

wagtails, dunlin, sanderlings, turnstones and ringed plover. Seals bob up from above the deep-blue water.

Tràigh Hough

Continue over the dunes, where there are many rows of small boulders. These were used for drying seaweed for kelp. Walk round the small bay of Tràigh Thallasgair, and then a bay full of pebbles. Head on to Dùn Hanais, a galleried dun. What wonderful sites our ancestors chose!

Press on along the beach, now Tràigh Thodhrasdail, with its great wall of creamy sand dunes, which lies below Kilkenneth. Towards the end of the beach, a large exposure of granite glows bright pink. Climb up onto the shallow dunes above Tràigh Ghrianal and saunter on, outside the fence. Pass through a gate and walk to where a mass of coltsfoot flowers. Step across Abhainn na Cille and begin to strike over the extensive greensward towards the road. Turn right to rejoin your car.

6. A Circular Walk around the West Coast of Coll

Information

Distance:	8½ miles
Time:	5-6 hours
Map:	Pathfinder 300 Coll (Arinagour), reference 152538 (parking)
Terrain:	Easy walking.

Keep dogs on leads at all times. All gates found closed must be closed after use. Please use stiles. Do not walk over seeded pastures, silage or hay fields.

Set out from Arinagour, an attractive village with a row of white-washed cottages provided in the 19th century by

Arinagour

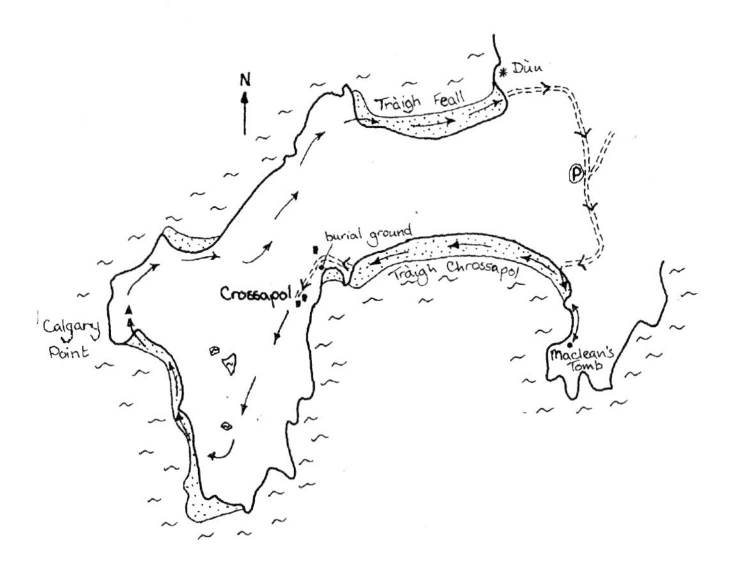

Alexander MacLean, the laird, for the workers on his estate.

Drive along the B8070 to Arileod, where you turn left. To view the two Breachacha Castles, turn left at the dwelling curiously named The Roundhouse. This is thought to be the site of a round watch tower for the original castle, but the tower was later replaced by a house.

Continue along the narrow road to view the castles over the intervening pastures. The 'Old Castle', nearer the shore, is white and magnificent and dates from the 15th century. In 1961 it was bought by Major Nicholas MacLean Bristol, a descendant of the MacLeans of Coll, who has restored it.

The 'New Castle', 18th century and dramatically turreted, was built for the chief of the Coll MacLeans. Here Dr Johnson and Boswell stayed.

Return to The Roundhouse, turn left and drive to the end of the road. Park on the sandy sward, beyond the cattle grid. This is part of the RSPB reserve.

Walk left (south), along the sandy track towards the mile-long stretch of golden sands, Tràigh Chrossapol. Turn left (east) and stroll a short way along the sands and then inland, heading for MacLean's Tomb. This is a dilapidated stone building, with twin turrets, guarding an arched doorway into the walled, but roofless, square enclosure. It was built in 1805 by Alexander MacLean for his wife, and he also was interred here later.

Return to the shore and head west along the glorious bay. Ahead, ringed plovers race over the sand and on the grassy sward dunlin feed. Press on around the graceful arc to take a track leading up over the dunes towards Chrossapol burial ground, which stands in front of a white house. Go inside the little cemetery, which looks out to the bay. If the grass has been cut, adding the scent of hay to the sights and sounds of the sea, all your senses are delighted. Sadly the waves are ravaging the burial ground's outer wall and it is beginning to tumble into the sea. Below, seals dally.

From the gate of the burial ground, turn left and continue along the track to pass through a gate by the refurbished Caolas House. Turn right, immediately, and climb the stile beside another gate. Go on, left, to walk with the hydro-poles to your right.

Press on, climbing stiles by gates, heading in the direction of the prominent post, bearing a large yellow diamond-shaped metal plate, which marks the submarine cable terminus. Once clear of the fences, bear right to stroll the beautiful twin bays

Ringed plovers and dunlin

of Caolas. Then head on towards the triangulation point (48 feet) on Calgary Point, a dramatic viewpoint of gneiss and granite.

Keep to the high ground as you walk north. Pass through the stiled fence and gradually bear away from the cliffs to continue ahead beside a fence on your right. Keep by this fence over the high pastures until you join a track by a large agricultural shed. Follow the track until it swings sharp right to an identical shed, and then walk ahead.

Proceed over the pasture, keeping parallel with a fence on your left. Here, you might come upon a flock of whimbrel feeding assiduously. Stay with the fence, as it swings left towards the edge of the dunes, and pass through a wooden gate to the lovely sands of Tràigh Feall. Go on along this wonderful stretch of gold, backed by towering sand dunes, some 50 feet high.

Leave the sands by a track over pastures and follow it right as it nears a fence. Stroll on to rejoin your car near the cattle grid.

7. A Circular Walk from Totronald, Coll

Information	
Distance:	$5\frac{1}{2}$ miles
Time:	2-3 hours
Map:	Pathfinder 300 Coll (Arinagour), reference 165558 (parking)
Terrain:	Easy walking.

Leave Aringour by the B8070. At the T-junction at Arileod, turn right. Drive on for just over half a mile and find a suitable parking space, not obstructing gates or passing places. Walk on to see two standing stones, possibly dating from the Iron Age, in a pasture on the right. These are named 'The Tellers of Tales'.

Continue down the hill to pass the RSPB warden's house in what was once Totronald Farmhouse. Beyond the end of the road lies a wide flat area, which was once used for sports gatherings and as a landing strip for planes. Listen for warblers in the nearby reed beds.

Bear left and follow the fence. Here, you might hear a corncrake calling from the long grass behind Totronald. Head towards the sea and the dunes and then past great whalebacks of gneiss. Pause at the highest point to enjoy the magnificent Tràigh Hogh, a wide curving bay of golden sand, over which flow deep turquoise rollers, topped with white foam. From here you can glimpse Rùm, the Uists and Barra. Descend over the turf (one vast mat of primroses in spring), and then the rocks to the bay. Walk where black-headed, herring and lesser black-backed gulls probe. To the right tower dunes over 50 feet high.

At the end of the bay, step across the stream, which flows out of Loch Ballyhaugh, and follow the fence to pass through a gate on the left. Stride the track ahead, keeping right of Ballyhaugh, the Hebridean Centre for the Project Trust, which places volunteers overseas. Pass through another gate to join a narrow road.

Walk beside the pleasing Loch Ballyhaugh, where a pair of mute swans nest. Further up the road, go through another gate. Above, on the left, are two thatched cottages. Stroll on to pass through, on the right, a gate that gives access to a track leading to a ruined croft. Behind stand several more ruins.

From the first ruin, follow the path ahead to a gap in the stone wall, and make your way between two gate stoops. Then climb to the summit of Ben Hogh (339 feet). Look for a huge boulder left perched on three small rocks by a receding ice flow. From the triangulation point there is a wonderful view of the three hills of Tiree, the island of Gunna between

Perched boulder

Tiree and Coll, Skerryvore Lighthouse, Eigg, Rùm, the Cuillin on Skye, Barra and the Uists. Further to the east, Ben Nevis and Ben Mor can be seen. Between the mainland and Coll, the Treshnish Islands seem to float on a navy-blue sea.

Return down the hill and turn left to walk past the loch and then the centre. Proceed along the track and pass through the gate. Turn left and climb the dunes, keeping parallel with the fence. From the corner, you can glimpse the loch. Follow the fence as it bears south. Here, the dunes are pitted with rabbit holes and the occupants sunbathe on grassy slopes. Look for dog lichen growing among the grass and a tiny pink cranesbill. Here, too, spurrey grows, and sandwort.

Corncrake in grass

When Totronald comes into view, head in that direction, descending to the flat sandy area. Here, among hollows, lie tranquil pools, where a hare lopes away. Here, too, green plovers wheel and dive. Grey-lag geese rise, cackling, as they are disturbed from their grazing. Continue ahead to join the road. Climb up it and then on to rejoin your car.

8. A Circular Walk around Cornaigbeg, North-East Coll

Information	
Distance:	2½ miles
Time:	2 hours
Map:	Pathfinder NM 26 Coll (North) reference 234628 (parking)
Terrain:	Easy walking.

This short walk takes you over sand dunes to the silvery beaches of north-east Coll. It returns you along the narrow B8072, where, at most times of the year, you are more likely to meet sheep and cattle than cars.

Ruined croft

Leave Arinagour by the B8071. At the crossroads, turn right and climb to Cranaig. To your left lies Gallanach, where once many hectares of bulbs grew. The road beyond Cranaig, not metalled until the 1920s, climbs through Windy Gap. Beyond and below lies Killunaig Chapel and graveyard, which you might like to visit.

Go on to park just before a gate across the road. Pass through and walk on, with a wonderful view of Eigg, Muck and the snow-covered tops of the Skye Cuillin through a gap in the mountains of Rùm. Continue on the road until you reach a track where you turn left. Head towards the shore beside a fence on your right.

The track leads you to a small sandy bay. Press on east along the shallow dunes, stepping across a narrow stream. Look for eiders, redshanks, oyster-catchers and hoodies. When you reach a fence between you and the shore, either move to the outside at its start, stepping over rocks just above high tide, or follow it round until you come to a hurdle in place of a gate. If the tide is out you might wish to visit the lovely green island, Eilean nan Uan.

Follow the contours round on the seaward side of the next area of high dunes, where a hare races away. There is a glorious view ahead. Go on along the deeply indented coastline, which has innumerable sandy pockets. Step across another stream and press on over great outcrops of gneiss (the way could be wet underfoot here) until you come to the side

Snipe and kingcups

of Cornaig Bay. Walk right, along its shoreline, following the fence to the road. Go with the fence until you reach a gate to the road. In the latter years of the 19th century, the bay was very busy, being used by east-coast fishermen for several months of the year.

Walk left (east), along the road. Here, a pair of snipe feed quietly among the milkmaids and kingcups in the roadside dyke. At the postbox, turn right to walk a track into Bousd. This was once a busy township, with over a hundred people. There was a school and a church. Today, two or three of the ruined houses have been restored; walk up the left fork of the track, beyond a refurbished cottage, to see the sad remains of ruined houses. Along the right fork, beyond another cottage, more roofless houses can be seen.

Return to the road, and turn left to walk back to rejoin your car.

9. A Linear Walk to Loch Fada, Coll

Information

Distance:	3 ½ miles
Time:	1 ½ hours
Map:	Pathfinder NM 26 Coll (North), reference 243631 (parking)
Terrain:	Can be wet. Good footwear essential.

This moorland walk is delightful, but choose good weather. It should not be attempted in mist. You might like to combine it with Walk 8.

Loch Fada

Pass through the gate on the B8072 (see Walk 8). Go by Cornaigbeg farmhouse on the right and park on the grass verge, just before the road becomes 'dual carriageway'. On the right side of the road is a wide grassy area. Walk across this to the row of hydro-poles. Climb the gneiss outcrops, left, following the poles. These lead you around a marshy area to a large startlingly-striped gneiss rock.

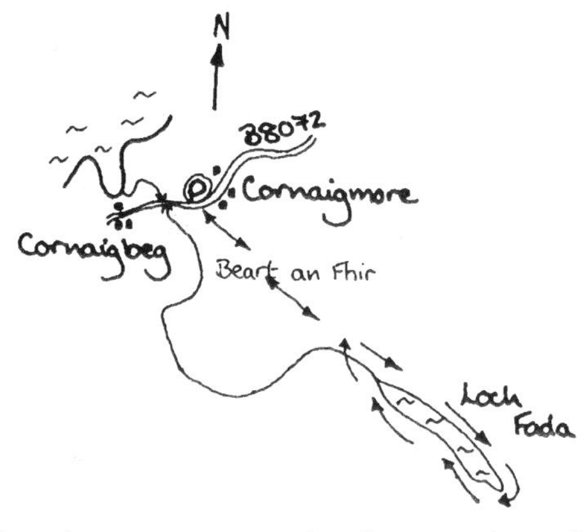

Bear right in the direction of the highest hill, Beart an Fhir (148 feet). Hug the left of this steep-sided hill. Look here for deep blue milkwort growing among the heather and bog myrtle. The narrow path, often indistinct, funnels you into a gully between rocky outcrops down which, after rain, hurries a stream. At the top, veer left and climb the highest outcrop on your right. From here you can see your aim, the lovely Loch Fada, lying in its rocky, moorland fastness.

Choose the driest way and climb another outcrop, as you go, to check that you are on course. Once at the loch continue right round its shoreline. Herons abound in this part of Coll, with its abundance of lochs. They can find few trees for nests, so they build on stunted outgrowths on islets.

Return by the same route, heading for the high hill used as a marker on your outward walk.

Milkwort

10. A Circular Walk from the Pier, Colonsay

Information	
Distance:	1 mile
Time:	1 hour
Map:	Pathfinder 375, NR 38/39/49 Colonsay, reference 394941 (parking)
Terrain:	Rough pasture; strong shoes advisable.

The harbour at Scalasaig is rather exposed and the pier, built in 1965, had to be strongly constructed with good fendering to withstand the pressure of the ferry in rough weather.

Paps of Jura from Scalasaig

From the harbour, walk ahead to visit Colonsay's heritage centre. Go on uphill, where the road is lined with flags to visit, also on the left, the Presbyterian church, a plain building full of peace. Then turn left into a wide track, beyond the church. Stride on, uphill, into the quiet moorland. Away to your right are two squat standing stones.

Leave the track and bear left along the ridge towards a tall granite memorial on a high mound, a good landmark for

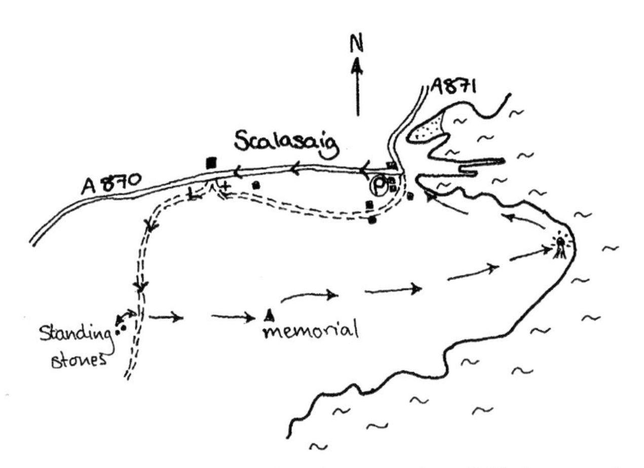

yachtsmen. It was raised by the people of Colonsay in honour of the Lord of Colonsay in the late 18th and early 19th century.

Go on in the same direction to descend the hill by a safe route and head towards the harbour lighthouse, gleaming white on the shoreline. Aromatic bog myrtle and bog asphodel line the route, so pick the driest way.

From the lighthouse, bear left, along the great whalebacks of rock, towards the harbour. Join the road, and turn right for the ferry.

11. A Circular Walk below Beinn Eibhne, Colonsay

Information	
Distance:	$3\frac{1}{2}$ miles
Time:	2 hours
Map:	Pathfinder 375, NR 38/39/49 Colonsay, reference 373911 (parking)
Terrain:	A delightful walk. Some paths along the shore might be wet, but pick the driest way.

Drive ahead from the pier at Scalasaig, and pass Colonsay Hotel on the right. After one-and-a-half miles, turn left along the A869 and continue to the end of the road, where you can park.

Walk back along the narrow road to take a reinforced track on the right. This climbs steadily through dwarf willow, bog myrtle, heather, rush and hard fern. Twites sit on the wire of fences, song thrushes fly into nearby bramble bushes and a heron wings slowly overhead.

Pair of twites

To the left lies Loch Cholla, which supports a glorious array of white water lilies. Then the Paps of Jura come into view, followed by Islay. Take the narrow footpath, right, to visit the monument to the McPhees, very early proprietors of Colonsay. A plaque says that in 1023 Malcolm, last chief of the McPhee clan, was murdered by a renegade MacDonald. Close by the monument are the ruins of a chapel and a burial ground.

Go on along the track to pass a house named Balerominmore. Walk the continuing track, which is sometimes indistinct. Go through a gate in a wall to step out onto the shore. Bear right. Here, the sward is a mass of low-growing thrift. As you continue, yellow bedstraw mingles with the pink flowers.

Stroll along the dunes to pass two lovely sandy bays. Here, a family of geese swims in a line on the wonderfully blue water. Continue round the low grassy cliffs, where English stonecrop flowers and basalt dykes stretch out to sea. Then as you walk, scuff your feet to hear the sands 'sing', as air, trapped between the sand grains is released - just as on the Isle of Eigg.

The Strand looking towards Oronsay

Across the narrow channel on your left lies the isle of Oronsay. Follow the contour round the slopes of Rubha Bàgh nan Capull and Rubha Dubh, both overlooking The Strand, the mile-wide stretch of tidal sand between Oronsay and Colonsay. Overshadowing all is Beinn Eibhne (240 feet). If the tide is out, cut across the sands to rejoin your car.

12. A Linear Walk to the Isle of Oronsay

Information

Distance:	5 miles
Time:	2 ½ -3 hours
Map:	Pathfinder 375, NR 38/39/49 Colonsay, reference 373911 (parking)
Terrain:	Easy walking - but check the time of the tides and leave yourself time to visit the priory and return safely, without getting wet.

Cloisters, St Columba's Priory

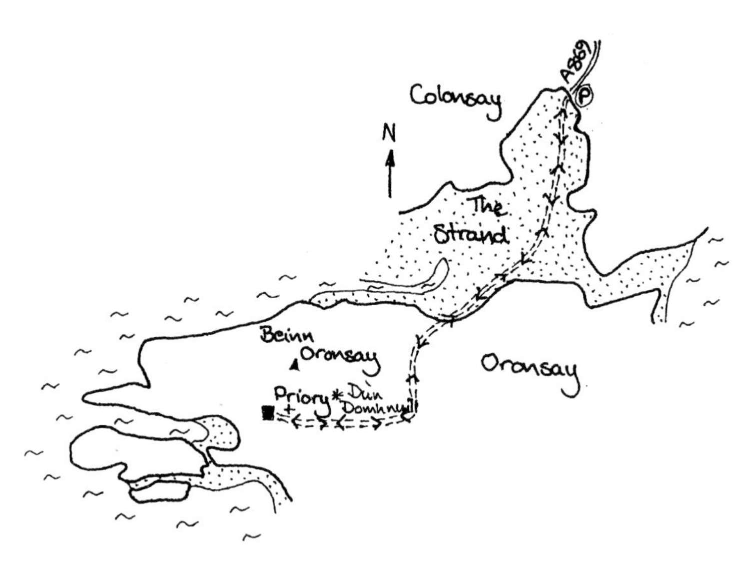

Oronsay is smaller that Colonsay and can be reached at low tide by walking across The Strand, a mile-wide stretch of tidal sand.

Park as for Walk 11, having first checked the tide tables at the hotel or the post office; The Strand can be crossed in walking boots or other footwear that you don't mind getting wet with seawater. You might get across almost dryshod. On a warm day it is fun to paddle.

Follow the vehicle tyre-marks - generally those of the post van - across the sands. You should aim for the tarmacked road on Oronsay, seen before you start but soon hidden behind rocks as you progress. The track across the sands first swings a little left from the end of road where you have parked, then bears right before coming close to low cliffs on Oronsay by a marker post encircled with yellow bands. The way continues right, close to the cliffs.

Here, the track becomes a tarmacked road. A notice says that all dogs must be on a lead. Go on for a mile through quiet moorland and then the hay meadows of Oronsay Farm. The road ends at the ruined Priory of St Columba, built in the 13th century on the site of a Celtic monastery. It is believed that the saint visited the island on his way from Ireland to Iona. As you pass through the gate to the lovely property, you see a small 6th-century cross set on a mound.

Look for the magnificent cross and the small cloisters. Visit the restored Prior's House, where magnificent tombstones stand around the walls and two effigies lie in the centre.

Buzzard on crag

Return by the same route and watch for a pair of buzzards and their young on the outcrops of Beinn Oronsay (230 feet).

13. A Circular Walk from the Pier across Colonsay's Rocky Spine

Information	
Distance:	5 miles
Time:	3 hours
Map:	Pathfinder 375, NR 38/39/49 Colonsay, reference 394941 (parking)
Terrain:	Easy walking all the way.

Leave the pier at Scalasaig, parking as for Walk 10, and walk straight ahead to the Colonsay Hotel. Just beyond the outbuildings, take the track, an old road, going off right. Pass the telephone exchange and then, on the right a standing stone set among smaller stones; the shape suggests a burial cairn. From here, there is a good view inland across the island.

Continue on where bog myrtle and heather cover outcrops of rock on Am Beannan. Pass through a gate over the track and go on.

After the steady climb to the top of the pass, descend the lovely track, with Beinn nan Gudairean to your left and Carn nam Caorach to your right. Just as Turraman Loch comes into view, look for the well to your right. On the drinking cup chained to a rock the inscription reads, 'Wish your will, drink your fill'. After the lengthy climb over the hill, once the only route, a drink from the well must have been most welcome.

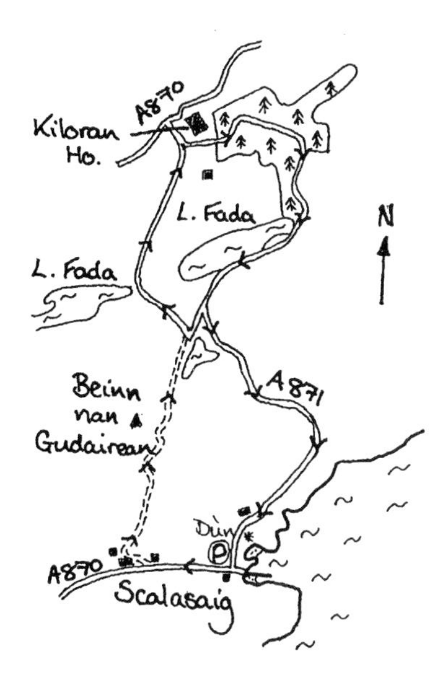

Stroll on downhill, passing the dam of the loch, where honeysuckle clambers over sycamore and hazel.

Emerge from the track onto a road, and turn left to pass a sheep dip on the right. Saunter on between two of the three lochs, all called Fada, once one continuous stretch of water. Here, in the reed beds, sedge and reed warblers call. Look left to the skyline above the westernmost Loch Fada, where between two white houses stand two very tall standing stones.

Stride on along the traffic-free road. Water avens, ragged robin and water buttercup all grow in the ditch. Twites sit on a nearby fence. In an elder tree covered with large white blooms a whitethroat perches, pouring forth its song.

Pass the village hall at Kiloran and, beyond, turn

Drinking cup chained to a rock

right to walk a reinforced track through the woodland of Colonsay House. Follow the arrowed sign for 'woodland and garden'. Go through the gate and take a narrow path right that leads to the pond, set amid quiet woodland. Then take another path, left, to return to the track again.

Walk the pleasing way, where great bushes of rhododendrons support huge colourful blossoms. These shrubs grow among a large variety of tall forest trees, many from foreign lands.

Just before a holiday cottage called Avenue, leave the track left for another pleasant diversion. This takes you along a cleared way between more rhododendrons. On regaining the track, stride on.

Beyond a buttressed wall on the left you have a glimpse of the delightful Colonsay House, which is not open to the public. Step out along along the track and follow it as it moves out onto moorland on one side and woodland on the other. Then the shady way continues, lined by trees on both sides. On the right, the northern end of the northernmost Loch Fada comes into view, with large white waxen water-lilies on its still blue water.

Water avens, ragged robin and spearwort

Pass through the gateless gap and onto open moor, with stranded cliffs to the left and the loch below to your right. At the metalled road you have a choice, either to turn right to join the old road taken earlier, or to turn left and return by the road to the pier.

All of Colonsay's roads are a delight to walk and as you climb the hill you have a glorious view of the Paps of Jura. Then Islay comes into view. After one-and-a-half miles, go past The Manse, with its colourful fuchsia hedge, then the modern surgery and the old post office, to return to the pier.

14. A Circular Walk to Ardskenish, Colonsay

Information

Distance:	6½ -7 miles
Time:	3 hours
Map:	Pathfinder 375, NR 38/39/49 Colonsay, reference 361938 (parking)
Terrain:	Easy walking. Scrambling over the rocks is helped by their roughness.

Leave Scalasaig by the A870 and travel west until you reach the golf course below Beinn nan Caorach. Park on the edge of the course and walk over the links towards the sands of Tobair Fhuair. Bear left and stroll around the bay, where pied wagtails race across the sand. Keeping close to the shoreline, clamber up the great whalebacks of sandstone. Watch out for the angry terns that dive at your head if they think you are intruding on their territory. Inland, on the machair, green plovers wheel and dive.

Continue over close-cropped turf, a wonderful flower garden in mid-summer. And then begin to clamber up the clearly-cairned Dùn Gallain, where the sketchy remains of an ancient fort stand. Take care as you walk round the perimeter wall of stones as the cliffs drop sheer to the sea far below. What an impregnable look-out for

Common terns

those ancient defenders.

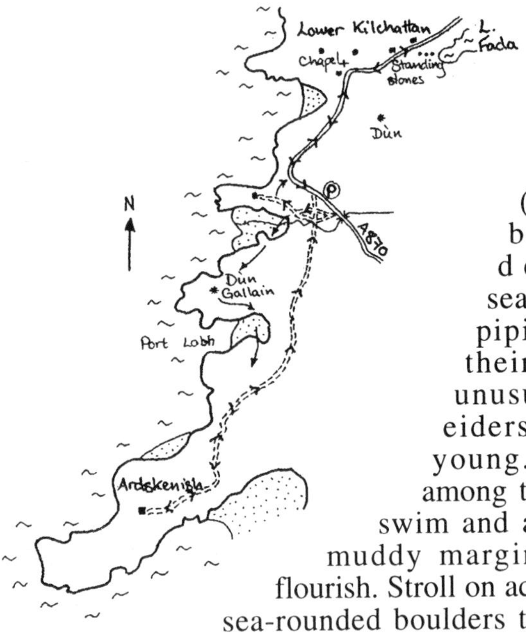

Go on round the cliffs, or cross the sand of Port Lobh (meaning Port Stink because of the decomposing seaweed). Here, rock pipits catch flies for their brood and, unusually, two male eiders marshal their young. In a small pool among the rocks, minnows swim and a snipe probes the muddy margins, where rushes flourish. Stroll on across a large field of sea-rounded boulders tossed there during earlier storms and high tides. The pretty silver weed and yellow bedstraw flower near the edges of the carpet of rocks.

Again, climb up the cliffs, keeping away from the extreme edges, which dramatically overhang the sea below. On the sward grows mountain everlasting. From here you can see the isles of Tiree and Coll.

Look landwards to see the farmhouse at Machrins. Join a good track, turn right and follow this delightful way through huge rocky outcrops. As the track approaches sand-dunes, look for a convenient sheltered ledge of rock to sit and sunbathe. Below, long fingers of black rock stretch out into the sea, dividing the shore into small sandy bays.

The track continues through a maze of sand-dunes, covered with spiky marram. It ends at the farmhouse at Ardskenish. Across the dunes you can see Beinn Oronsay and, beyond, the Paps of Jura.

Return along the track, below the rocky outcrops, and then over moorland. Go on over the golf links, which are used as an emergency landing strip. Cross a stream by a plank and walk on to pass through a gate. Stride the good track. As you near your car, keep left (west) of the hill on top of which perches the coastguard lookout, and then join the road.

Stride on the quiet way to Lower Kilchattan, one of the island's three villages. Visit the graveyard, with its ruined chapel. Climb up the hill, passing the track to Seaview Farm. Look over the next gate on the right to see the tall standing stones glimpsed on the last walk. Visit the stones only if the hay has been cut, to avoid damage to the crop. Stand by the gate and listen for corncrakes in the fields about the graveyard and the farm.

Ardskenish

Walk back along the road, from where there are good views of Port Mór. Rejoin your car.

15. A Linear Walk from Kiloran Bay to Balnahard Bay, Colonsay

Information	
Distance:	6 miles
Time:	3 hours
Map:	Pathfinder 375, NR 38/39/49 Colonsay, reference 398976 (parking)
Terrain:	Easy walk apart from the steep climb soon after joining the reinforced track.

Kiloran Bay, a glorious symmetrical curve of golden sand backed by grass-topped dunes, lies between Beinn an Sgoltaire and Carnan Eoin (360 feet), Colonsay's highest hill. To reach this delightful part of the island, leave the pier at Scalasaig and turn right to drive the narrow A871 through the island, taking the A870 right at the T-junction to head towards the sands, where the road ends. There is a small parking area here.

Kiloran Bay

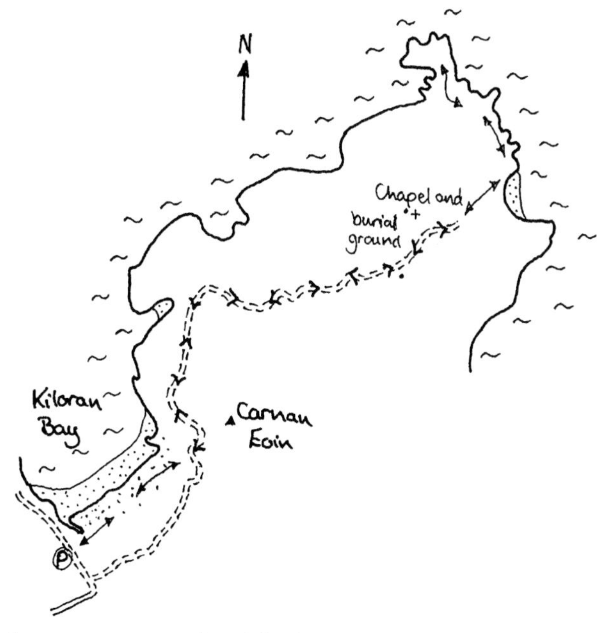

Drop down to a wooden kissing-gate, which gives access to the dunes and the sands. Continue north over the dunes, which are alive with skylarks and meadow pipits. Join a good track also leading north. A steep climb takes you uphill, passing below Carnan Eoin. Then follow a high flat part of the way before descending to cross one of Colonsay's many raised beaches.

Keep to the good track as it swings inland, first through heather moorland and then the pastures about Balnahard farmhouse. Just before the farmstead stands a circular building, pleasingly restored, where horses once turned millstones to grind the grain. Above the farm on a rocky ledge of Beinn Bhreac sits a young eagle and overhead circles one of the adults.

Look for the standing stone to the left and then continue to the barn at the end of the reinforced track. Climb the stile and walk the path over the flower-covered machair until you reach the enchanting bay - a delight to swim in but colder than most on the island.

Before returning, you may like to take the opportunity to walk to the northernmost tip of Colonsay. From the bay, head north, delighting in the wonderful sea air and the lovely views as Mull comes into sight.

Enjoy the peace and isolation before retracing your steps to rejoin your car.

Circling eagle

16. A Circular Walk from Salen, Mull

Information

Distance: 4½ miles
Time: 2½ hours
Map: Pathfinder NM 44/54 Salen, reference 572433 (parking)
Terrain: Easy walking all the way.

This is a good family walk but note well that the ruins are in a precarious state.

Salen lies ten miles south of Tobermory and is reached by the A848, a narrow road with passing places. Park close to the public toilets.

General Lachlan MacQuarrie, born on Mull, founded the village. Later, he became governor of New South Wales. He eventually returned to Mull and, when he died in 1824, was buried in a large mausoleum at Gruline, two miles south-west of Salen.

Walk along the A848, in the direction of Tobermory, for half a mile. The road hugs the shore, where eiders float and sandpipers call from rocks. Cross the road and take a kissing-gate beside a gate that has a notice, 'No Dogs'. Climb the gently ascending track through the trees, where in spring

Sandpiper on rocks

the woodland floor is a mass of primroses, violets, wood sorrel, wood anemone, bluebells, celandines and golden saxifrage.

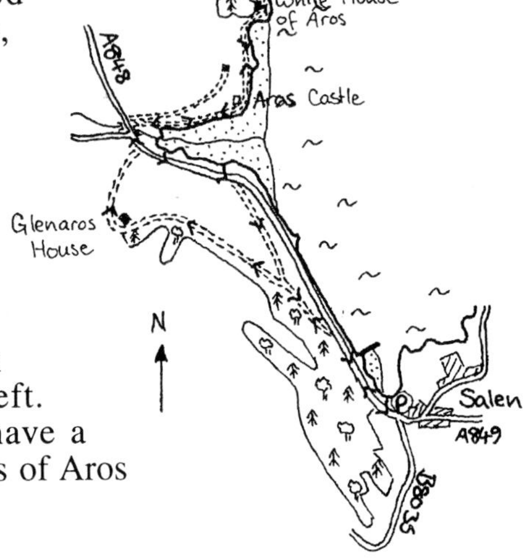

When the trees cease on your right, enjoy the glorious view of the Sound of Mull. Pass through the next gate and walk on beside a wall on your left. From this pasture you have a dramatic view of the ruins of Aros Castle.

Walk to the left of Glenaros House to join a narrow metalled road. Turn right and begin the steady descent. Look for a delightful waterfall, cascading through the deciduous woodland on your left. From these trees come the calls of willow warbler, wren, cuckoo and green woodpecker.

At the road end, cross the A848 and walk over a green sward to a delightful old stone bridge spanning the Aros River. Once over the bridge, turn right to walk (there is no right of way for cars) the narrow track that edges the glorious shore. Continue as the track winds below the ruins of Aros Castle and press on to beyond the White House of Aros, at one time an inn. Here, the lovely way ends at a small pier, once the main one for Mull.

Return along the track and take the first right turn, up through trees, to the 13th-century castle. From the stark ruins there is a wonderful view of the Sound and Salen Bay. In 1608, Hebridean chiefs were invited to the castle. They were later asked to dine on the flagship *Moon,* belonging to Lord Ochiltree, the Lieutenant of the Isles. Once they had dined, they were kidnapped. Then they were imprisoned in various places in Scotland for more than a year, until they had sworn loyalty to the House of Stuart.

Aros Bridge

Descend from the castle by a narrow path to the right of the ruins, through bluebell and bracken, to the track by the shore. Turn right and return over the old stone bridge. Cross the A848 and walk left, with care, for 400 yards, to take the second track leading off right.

Climb the pleasing way, passing through two gates, and at the boundary wall walk right and then left through a gate taken earlier. Retrace your outward route to rejoin your car.

17. A Circular Walk from Tobermory, Mull

Information	
Distance:	2½ miles
Time:	2 hours
Map:	Pathfinder 302, NM 45/55 Tobermory, reference 505551 (parking)
Terrain:	Easy walking. Path through woods can be muddy after rain.

The bright red, blue, pink and cream houses that line the gracefully curving bay of Tobermory give the walker a warm welcome. Allow yourself time to enjoy the many small shops before you set off to the lighthouse, Rubha nan Gall, and the hill of Druim Nead an Fhireoin (280 feet).

Birch

Park in the free car park, close to the harbour, at the southern end of the small town. Walk along Main Street to Caledonian MacBrayne's pier and take the reinforced track, which ascends steadily through deciduous woodland. Continue along the pleasing high-level way. Wooded slopes climb steeply above you and drop steeply to the shore. Parts of this path require careful walking, particularly if you are accompanied by children.

Stroll along the lovely path, where in spring a myriad of flowers bedecks the way. Follow it as it leads out of the trees

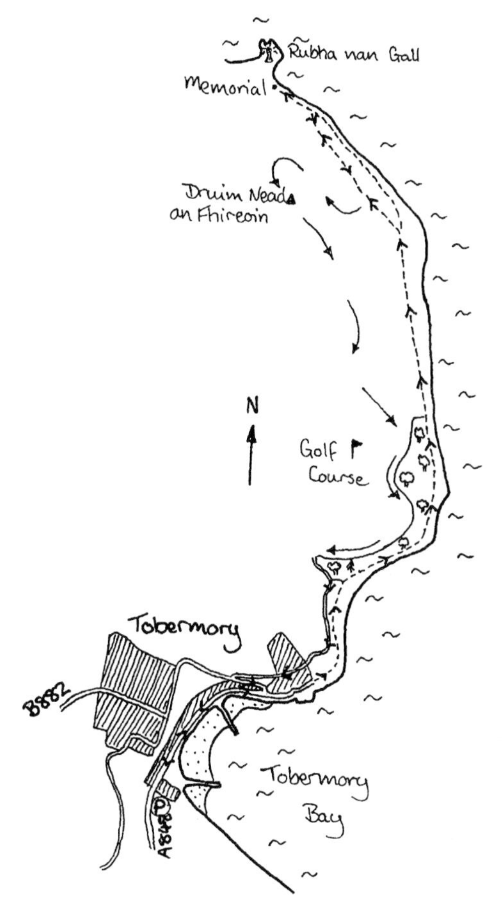

and on along the cliffs, with a magnificent view of the Sound of Mull, Loch Sunart and Morvern on the mainland. Keep to the lower path as it descends through more birch to come to a memorial to Robert John Brown of Tobermory. Sit on the seat and use the viewfinder to identify the breathtaking scene. Ahead lies the lighthouse, Rubhna nan Gall, automated in the 1960s, a hundred years after it was built.

Climb the steep rough track, known as Jacob's Ladder, that leaves the main path close to the memorial. Continue to a division of tracks through the bracken, where you take the right branch. Bear right to pass, on your left, several ruined houses. Then take the first track left, which leads up to the cairn on Druim Nead an Fhireoin. Enjoy this magnificent viewpoint, from where you can see Calve Island, which guards the entrance to Tobermory Bay and makes it a safe anchorage.

Stroll the clear path and descend over heather moorland. Follow the way as it swings right towards a sturdy fence onto Tobermory golf course. Here a notice welcomes walkers 'at their own risk', and you are asked to follow the green-topped posts, keep to the sides of the fairways and avoid disrupting play.

Tobermory

The posts take you on a delightful route around the course and bring you to a white iron gate onto a track. Bear left and follow it to join a metalled road, where you turn left. Pass the war memorial and stride on. At the road junction, turn left and then right to rejoin Main Street and to return to your car.

18. A Circular Walk along the Cliffs overlooking Loch Tuath, Mull

Information	
Distance:	9 miles
Time:	5-6 hours
Map:	Pathfinder NM 44/54 and NM 24/34, reference 396458 (parking)
Terrain:	Generally easy walking. Occasionally a head for heights is needed.

This is a pleasing walk along a lovely coastline, with spectacular views of Ben More and lesser heights. It is virtually pathless, but there are many sheep trods that go in the right direction. Half of the walk is along the narrow road, B8073, from which you obtain good views.

Park opposite Kilninian Church, Torloisk. Before you start, visit the church, which was built in 1755 on the site of an earlier one. The exterior has not been altered, although the interior has been refurbished. Leave by the side door and go into the vestry, on your left, to see a fine collection of medieval gravestones.

Return to the narrow road and turn left to walk east, for nearly two miles. Pass Torloisk House, with its splendid turreted roof, set amid trees. Go on past the cottages of Achleck and then Norman's Ruh. Next, pass two cottages on the left, followed by a ruined house on the right. Beyond, go

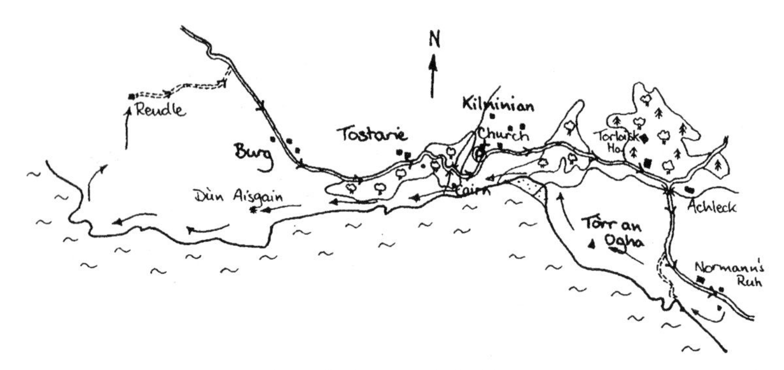

through a gate on the right and follow a grassy way that swings right, round the corner of the ruin. Keep right across the pasture to a stile over the fence. Walk ahead to cross the next stile and continue to a track that goes downhill to a sturdy pier jutting into Rainich Bay.

Ignore the way to the pier and turn right to climb the reinforced track. Where it zig-zags right, strike off left along a grassy way. Follow it as it continues to climb through a rocky gully onto a hill, Torr an Ogha, which you cross. Descend through another short rocky gully and follow the path as it swings right, inland, towards a footbridge over the Allt a' Mhuilinn and a large sheep dip. Once over the footbridge, bear left. Step across a small stream and walk on to join a track coming in on your right. Follow it towards the shore and then cross another footbridge.

Go on above the delightful sands of Tràigh na Cille. Watch out for the point where a sheep trod leads you into wind-blown birches. Step across a stream and head uphill, right, to pass through a gate in the fence. Continue along the high-level pastured way and then swing inland between grassy knolls, where you can glimpse Kilninian Church. Bear left and stride on.

Look for a dome-shaped pile of rocks. Follow the narrow path to cross a tiny stream and pass through a gate in the fence. Walk on towards a derelict wall, with a new fence beyond. Go through the gate, keeping to the path as it leads into scattered thorn and birch, close to the shore. Again, look

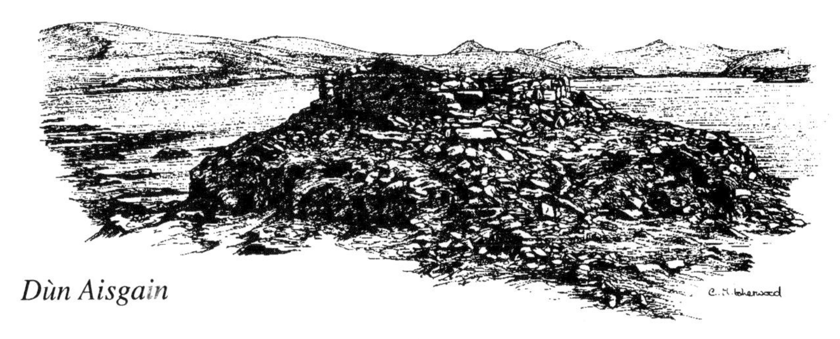

Dùn Aisgain

for a narrow path that leads steadily upwards through extensive oak woodland, the haunt of willow-warblers.

Step across yet another small stream and press on. Once out of the trees, go over pasture that covers a raised beach, with stranded cliffs to your right. Negotiate another stream, taking care - the boulders can be slippery. Head seawards towards a cairn on your left from where there is a wonderful view over the loch and towards the islands of Ulva and Gometra.

Look west for your first sighting of Dùn Aisgain and then descend to a gate in the fence. Before climbing upwards to explore the fortification, look at the many remains of the ruined village of Burg. This is the place to return to, to continue the walk after visiting the dun.

The dramatic galleried Iron-Age fort stands on an eminence, with a commanding view of the loch. It has thick walls and several lintels.

Return downhill to the ruined village and continue along a glorious stretch of raised beach. From the lovely path, look down with care on the shore far below, where eiders bask, and shags and cormorants perch on rugged rocks. The way goes on and on and then swings inland as it approaches the sea outlet of the Allt Reudle.

Here, a decision has to be made on how to rejoin the road to Kilninian. You may prefer to return along the high-level easy-to-walk way to the ruined village at Burg and then follow the fence (on your right) inland. This brings you to the modern

Shags and a cormorant

houses at Burg. Or you may wish to cross the Allt Reudle at a suitable crossing and continue upwards on the far side of the burn to the white house. From here a good track leads to the road, where you turn right to walk to Burg.

Beyond Burg stride the narrow road to pass the houses at Tostary. Begin to descend the twisting way and after the first S-bend look right to see a standing stone in a pasture. Stroll on to rejoin your car close to the church.

19. A Walk on the Isle of Ulva, close to the West Coast of Mull

Information

Distance:	10 miles
Time:	5-6 hours
Map:	Pathfinder 328, NM 33 Ulva; use map in Visitor's Guide
Terrain:	Easy walking, unless you leave the paths and tracks.
Refreshments:	At tearoom.
Public Transport:	Foot passengers only; bikes can be taken.

All dogs on leads - no dogs April and May (lambing time). Walking boots and outdoor clothing essential.

The magical day begins on Mull awaiting the ferry to Ulva. To summon the ferry, uncover a red board on the side of a building on the small pier. The ferry takes one minute to cross the Sound of Ulva. Then step onto an island where time stands still - at least for visitors.

Before setting off, call in at the interpretative museum above the tearoom. You can obtain excellent homemade food in the latter - and oysters and wine!

There are five walks of varying length, all sensitively signposted and waymarked with white painted stones and plain wooden posts. Visitors can follow these or are invited to blaze their own trail. The island has no tarmacked roads. The following walk combines a visit to see the basalt columns and

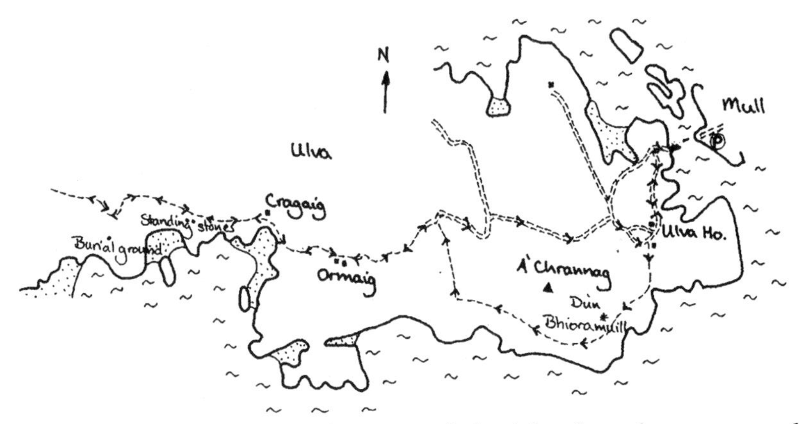

continues along the south coast of the island to the graveyard at Kilvekewan.

Leave the boathouse and tearoom and walk along a reinforced track to a six-armed signpost. Bear left for the basalt rocks, passing beside the glorious deciduous woodland of Ulva House. The house was built in the 1950s on the site of a large, early 19th-century house, destroyed by fire.

Ignore the turning for the woodland walk and continue towards Bracadale Farm. Just before the outbuildings, follow the signpost to walk left along a walled track and out onto open pasture towards the sea. Press on through the next gate which brings you out onto a small headland, with a grand view across Loch na Keal.

Inland, on the site of an old fort, Dùn Bhioramuill, stands the burial ground of the Clark family. The huge marble

Cliffs of basalt

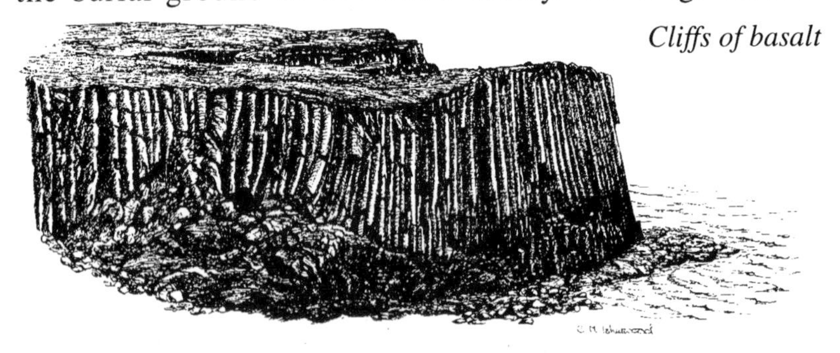

monuments lie inside a high gateless wall. Sir Francis Clark bought Ulva in 1835 and, while the kelp industry throve, cared well for the island's community of 600 people in 16 villages. Then the potato blight struck and the islanders had no employment or food. Clark tried various relief works but they all failed. By 1851 the population was reduced to 150 - it is now 25. Crofters were sent to North America or Australia, their passages paid for by the Emigration Society and the laird. The Clarks owned Ulva for 110 years.

Visiting the memorial involves a rather difficult scramble.

Look here, too, seaward, to see the basalt columns. These were formed when a volcano near Ben More, on Mull, poured forth layer after layer of molten lava. Glacial action resulted in the terraced landscape that you see so clearly on this south side of Ulva, and in the basalt columns - the result of the lava cooling quickly and crystallising.

Follow the path past lines of lazy-beds, where potatoes were grown in raised areas on soil taken from either side. To the right of the path, up a slope, tucked into the base of a high basalt-stranded cliff, is Livingstone's Cave. Here, 200 years ago, the father and grandfather of the missionary and explorer David Livingstone lived while waiting for a croft house. Enjoy the wonderful view they enjoyed. Previous ancient occupants left shells, flint artefacts and bones.

The way now descends to a large grassy area about which are scattered the ruins of several houses. From above the marshy ground comes the drumming of a snipe. Cross a ditch and climb a small slope to see a house similar to the one the Livingstone family would have lived in - again with a dramatic view from the doorway.

Follow the path, which now turns inland and climbs steadily through birch woodland; where walls, trees and boulders all support a thick layer of moss. At the top of the slope, join a track that continues to climb as it swings left. Stride on, enjoying the magnificent views out to sea. Then, begin to descend towards the ruined village of Ormaig, which has more lazy-beds about it.

Stroll on to the head of a small muddy tidal inlet to see an old cruck mill. Two large millstones lie on the grassy floor. Watch for heron and shelduck, feeding in the tidal gutter. Overhead, you might see an eagle mobbed by a pair of angry ravens or a kestrel pestered by bullying hoodie crows, the only hostility you are likely to witness on the island.

Walk on along the path, which brings you to the ruined village of Cragaig, where even more houses crowd the lovely slopes below the sheltering cliffs.

Kestrel and hoodie

As you pass two standing stones away to your left, look out towards several small islands, where many seals bask. Then continue to the ruined village of Kilvekewan. Drop down the slopes, seaward, to visit the ruined graveyard, where several MacQuarries are buried. General Lachlan MacQuarrie (see Walk 16) was the most famous member of the clan that had possessed the island for centuries. In 1773 he entertained Dr Johnson and James Boswell. In 1777 Lachlan had to sell Ulva to pay his debts.

Return along the track to the place where you joined it above the birch wood. Look for a standing stone in the pastures below and, beyond, over the Sound, enjoy a good view of the Eas Fors waterfall, plummeting magnificently over the cliff. Go on along the well signposted track to the pier, perhaps with just enough time for refreshments, before taking the last ferry to Mull.

20. A Circular Walk from Ardtun, Mull

Information

Distance:	4 miles
Time:	2½ hours
Map:	Pathfinder 341, NM 22/32 Iona and Bunessan, reference 383230 (parking)
Terrain:	Can be a wet walk - you may prefer to return by outward route.

This walk starts from a quiet corner, north of Bunessan, on the Ross of Mull. It continues round a lonely headland, where the way is pathless, except for sheep tracks, and can be wet. Towards the end it passes through woodland, in spring alive with the songs of migrants. It is an exhilarating walk and will be enjoyed by those who enjoy a challenge.

Leave Bunessan by the narrow road signposted Ardtun and park near the first left turn. Stride the left turn to walk above Tràigh Mhór, which is a mass of seaweed-covered black boulders at low tide. Look for sandpipers, oyster-catchers, rock pipits, green plover, eider, shelduck and whimbrel.

Pair of stonechats

Just before the last two cottages, where the road swings left, walk ahead over pasture, which soon becomes moorland. Once over the brow, Dùnan Mór lies ahead, a flat-

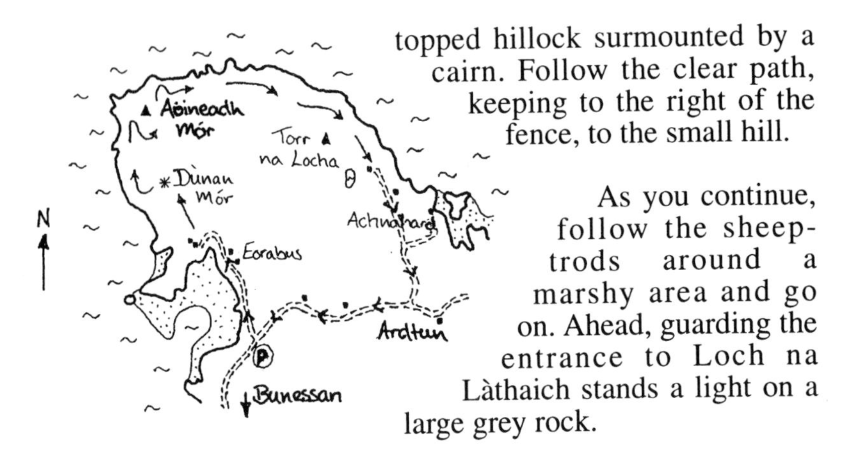

topped hillock surmounted by a cairn. Follow the clear path, keeping to the right of the fence, to the small hill.

As you continue, follow the sheep-trods around a marshy area and go on. Ahead, guarding the entrance to Loch na Làthaich stands a light on a large grey rock.

Follow the sheep-trods downhill to an extensive grassy area, where the ruins of several houses lie. Here, you may see a long-legged hare and a pair of stonechats. Walk to the edge of the low cliffs for a wonderful view of the columnar basalt, which here lies vertically and horizontally and also forms rosette patterns. Beyond the ruined houses and the magnificent basalt rears Aoineadh Mór, a great rocky headland. Out to sea you can glimpse Staffa.

Do not continue to the headland but look for a dry, rock-strewn gully in the shallow cliffs. Here can be found fossil-leaf beds, thin layers sandwiched between basalt - eroded by fossil hunters. A variety of wild flowers grow in this sheltered ravine.

Walk inland and climb the sheep trod through a breach in the stranded cliffs, behind the ruined houses. Walk left to continue around the high headland, the territory of ravens. From now on follow the coastline, keeping to sheep trods through the heather, avoiding as much of the wet moorland as possible. Across Loch Scridain lies the magnificent Ardmeanach headland - perhaps Mull's wildest scenery.

Go on beyond the fence. Look here for deep-blue milkwort. Do not be tempted to cut across the moorland to the side of Torr na Locha but continue around the heather-edged headland to a gap in a wall. Cross the top of a grassy gully running down to a small beach. Follow the sheep trods to pass through a gate in the next wall. Press on, keeping to the right side of the continuing ruined wall. Away to the right you can see Loch a' Chrionain. Below the wooded south side of Torr na Locha, stand several ruined cottages.

Ben More

The way continues along a gated track about which grow willow, rowan and honeysuckle. Here, a sedge warbler sings noisily. Pass another ruined cottage and stride on through more woodland alive with birds. Then the way becomes tarmacked. At the T-junction, turn right and stroll on to rejoin your car.

21. A Circular Walk on the Isle of Iona

Information	
Distance:	7½ miles
Time:	5-6 hours
Map:	Pathfinder 341, NM 22/32 Iona and Bunessan
Terrain:	Generally easy walking. Take care on the cliffs if windy.

This walk visits the sites associated with St Columba and the coming of Christianity to Britain. It takes you over the high moors, with their huge outcrops of Torridon sediments, to visit a fascinating disused marble quarry, and then continues to St Columba's Bay, where the saint landed in 563 AD. It returns past a brilliant blue loch before descending to cross an enormous stretch of sandy machair, which edges the Bay at the Back of the Ocean, the one big bay of the island. The walk also takes in a visit to the austere and magnificent St Mary's Abbey, and finally descends Dùn I, Iona's highest hill, for an overall view of the island and others beyond.

Iona lies a mile off the Ross of Mull. A regular Caledonian MacBrayne ferry service takes you from Fionnphort, at the end of the Ross, across the Sound of Iona. Ahead from the pier is The Village, where most of the island's population lives. Bear left to pass a toilet block, then Martyrs' Bay Restaurant and Finlay Ross's shop. Stride the metalled road and follow it as it swings uphill and

Wheatear

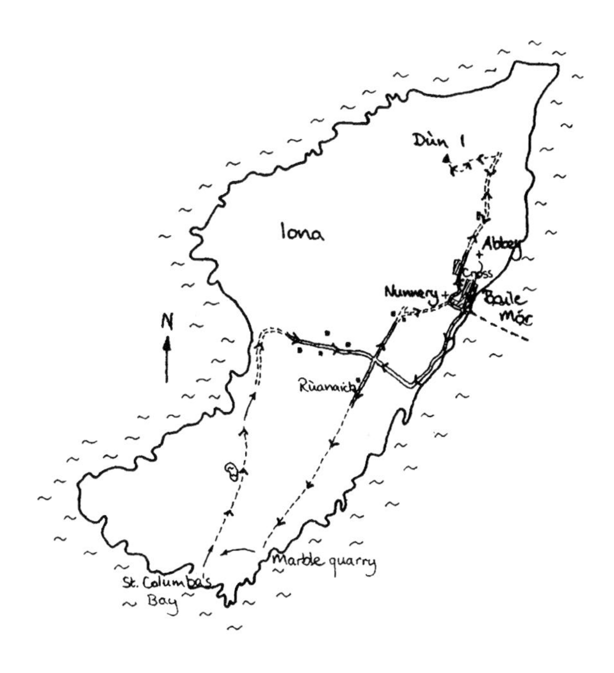

inland. At a crossroads, turn left to walk a track that leads past a white house named Ruanaich on the Ordnance Survey map.

Beyond, the track deteriorates as it climbs to a gate, which gives access to the slopes. Follow the well-worn way to the ridge and then bear slightly left to walk ahead, remaining on the high moorland. Below, there are glimpses of tiny sandy inlets. Follow a narrow path through a vast area of heather, colourful and sweet-smelling in August, and, in spring, resounding to the songs of skylarks, meadow pipits and wheatears.

Away to the right, you can see a fence marching parallel with the path you are following. When the fence turns left, stroll on for 400 yards towards the southern end of the island. Look for a grassy gully that runs gently downwards towards the sea. It takes you to the marble quarry. If you miss this and begin to bear west, glimpsing the pebbles of St Columba's Bay ahead, retrace your steps.

At the bottom of the gully you come to a grassy flat area, which is very wet but looks deceptively dry. On your right stand the foundations of two huts. These were used by quarry workers. Continue on to come to the edge of the quarry, where you can see the machinery used until quarrying ended in 1914. As you drop gently down, look left to see a tiny reservoir of water used to provide power for the machinery. Notice the robust tanks, engine and cutting frame. Wander around to see other artefacts left just where they were being used. Beyond is a litter of blocks, cut ready for shaping. Clamber over these and look down to see the steep-sided outcrop against which a small boat, carrying coke for the quarry's engine, would have unloaded. The dressed marble would have been taken away by the same boat.

Return to the ruined huts and swing left (west) picking the driest way, to continue to St Columba's Bay. This remote southern tip of the island is a very important place to Christians. Look for semi-precious stones, polished and rounded by the pounding of the sea.

From the beach, walk inland along a path through a grassy valley, with high outcrops on either side. This sometimes muddy way, which is carried by low footbridges over the worst areas, brings you to the east side of Loch Staoineig, used as a reservoir. Follow the clear track, which soon begins to descend towards the magnificent, extensive machair that edges the Bay at the Back of the Ocean and is the site of Iona's golf course. This is a glorious vista of white shell-sand, bright green grass, and a turquoise sea, which soon shades to purple as the water deepens.

Stroll on until you reach the right branch of the track, which you take. Beyond a gate, a metalled road continues and brings you to the crossroads where you turned left at the start of the walk. Turn left, this time to return to The Village. Press on along the reinforced track, which is flanked with irises. Follow it to a gate to a tarmacked road, where you turn right. Go past the next left turn to enter the 12th-century nunnery, which is one of Scotland's most attractive ruins. Several gables stand tall, and the pink, black and white granite used in the building supports the pretty pinky-blue ivy-leaved toadflax.

Leave by the gate in the far left corner and walk on to pass the heritage centre and then Iona's Church of Scotland, designed by Thomas Telford. On the roadside stands the grand medieval MacLean's Cross.

Just before St Mary's Abbey is St Oran's Chapel and cemetery, where lie the bones of 60 kings. - Scots, Irish,

St Mary's Abbey

Norse and French. Duncan and Macbeth are both buried here. The very small chapel is built of pink granite. The Christian burial ground is the oldest in Scotland.

Go on to visit the Abbey. It dates from the 13th century, but has been extensively restored in this century. The restoration commenced in 1938 and was completed in 1965. It is probably built on the site of St Columba's 6th-century monastery. The abbey and its surrounds are open to the public and in the summer it is visited by many modern-day pilgrims. The abbey community plays a vital part in the life of the island.

Inside, look for a huge slab of white marble, tinged with green, used as the altar table. It came from the quarry visited earlier. Notice the effigies of the Duke of Argyll and his wife. Stay as long as you wish in the quietness of the Abbey, and its cloisters with its bronze sculpture, and then continue along the road. Once past a white painted house on the right and another opposite, pass through a metal gate beyond, on your left. Keep on the track towards the large mass of Dùn I (pronounced Dùn Ee) and follow the path where it swings left, and then climbs steadily to the summit cairn (332 feet). From here you can see much of the island. Return from the summit by your outward route.

22. A Circular Walk from Craignure, Mull

Information

Distance:	2 miles
Time:	1 hour
Map:	Pathfinder 330, NM 63/73 Duart Point (Mull), reference 723367 (parking)
Terrain:	Easy walking.

This delightful short walk starts with a stroll along a forest ride leading to Torosay Castle, and returns through gracious parkland and over Druim Mór, a grassy ridge with breathtaking views.

Park in a lay-by by the castle's north lodge. If this is full, park in Craignure and walk south to the lodge. Stroll the ride beneath an avenue of sycamore and beech, where a golden warbler sings its pleasant song.

Climb gently to a white signpost and go on. High overhead you might see a golden eagle, quite stationary, resting on the upwelling air currents. Pass through a gate to enter the forest. It has a preponderance of conifers but also delightful pockets of deciduous trees. In areas where the trees have been felled, foxgloves provide a splendid show in mid-summer. Look for the seat well-placed to provide views, through a gap

Foxgloves

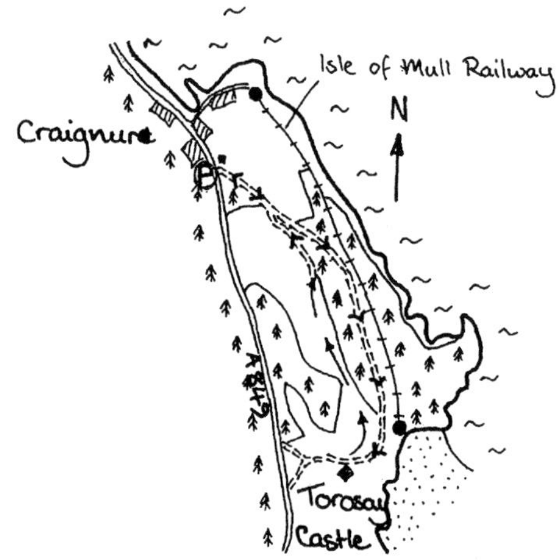

in the trees, of Duart Castle, perched on its crag at Duart Point. Stroll on to look down on the station of the Isle of Mull narrow-gauge railway. The journey from Craignure to Torosay, by diesel or steam, takes 20 minutes.

Beyond the next gate, you have your first view of Torosay Castle, and the track ahead leads to it. You may wish to visit the lovely house, designed by David Bryce in the Scottish Baronial style in 1858. Or perhaps you have time to stroll the 12 acres of garden laid out by Sir Robert Lorrimer in 1900. The Italianate terraces and the statue walk should not be missed.

From the castle, you may prefer to return by the railway. If however you wish to continue this circular walk, climb the stile opposite the castle shop. Ascend the gently-sloping pasture to a gate in the boundary fence to the right of a small wood. Continue beside woodland on your right to the top of Druim Mór, where a glorious view of the sound and of the mainland awaits. Drop steadily downhill to join a road on the right and stroll on to the forest road, taken at the outset of the walk, to rejoin your car.

Statue, Torosay Castle

23. A Walk on Staffa

Information

Distance:	2 miles
Time:	As much time as you are allowed by the condition of the sea.
Map:	Pathfinder 328, NM 33 Ulva (not necessary)
Terrain:	Easy grassy walking. Any wet areas have duckboards. Take care near the cliff edges when watching puffins. Concentrate as you walk along the roped causeway; some rocks can be slippery. Wear warm clothing and strong shoes. Carry a little food and drink.

Book the day before and check the trip is on before setting off.

The uninhabited island of Staffa lies seven miles off the west coast of Mull. Less than a mile long and about a third of a mile wide, Staffa's neighbouring islands are Gometra and Little Colonsay. Its famous landmark, Fingal's Cave, is inextricably linked with Mendelssohn's Hebridean Overture.

Hexagonal perpendicular basalt columns, set on a tufa base, rear up on either side of the yawning cavern. Above these columns, the columnar basalt lies horizontally. The cave is 228 feet long and 66 feet high. Other huge caves, Boat, The Great Face, Clamshell and Cormorant, pierce the dramatic cliffs.

This wonderful geological marvel has attracted many famous visitors, including Keats, Wordsworth, Sir Walter Scott, J.M.W. Turner, Queen Victoria and Prince Albert.

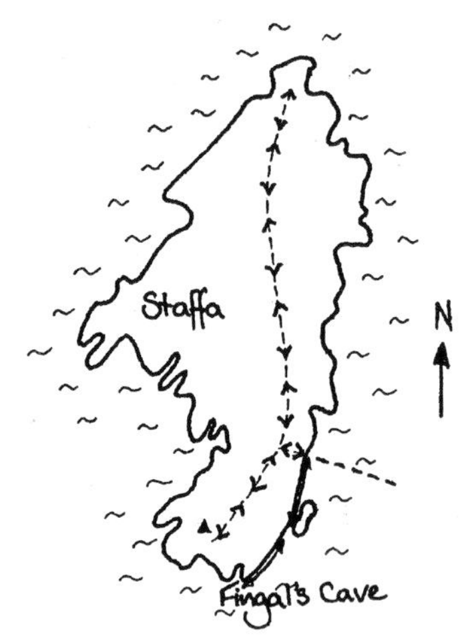

Boswell and Johnson viewed the island but were unable to land.

Today there are boat trips from Oban, Tobermory, Iona and Ulva. Look for seals, basking on the skerries, and for dolphins playing round the boat. You might see whales and porpoises. As you approach the little island, great rafts of puffins bounce up and down on the waves.

If the sea is calm, you land at a concrete jetty by Clamshell Cave. From it, when the tide is on the ebb, you walk left over a natural causeway below the towering basalt, with a rope to assist you on the landside and the white-topped waves licking the hexagonal rocks to your left. This leads to the yawning entrance of Fingal's Cave where the booming of the pounding waves echoes deafeningly.

Return to the jetty and climb the strong ladder up onto Staffa's grassy top. Turn right and walk the narrow path over the sward. The way climbs several shallow hills and from these you have wonderful views to the Treshnish Isles, Tiree, Coll and Mull. Approach the edge of the cliffs quietly. In May

Puffins

and June, the puffins will allow you near their burrows. Pairs sit at the entrances and court, with much stroking of their large bills. Some are busy inside and pop out at the approach of a mate. Others take off or return, extending their comical red legs and feet to make a perfect landing. Life is never still in a puffin colony. Towards the far end (north-east), steps drop down to a sheltered sea gully where landings can be attempted, when the swell is too strong for using the jetty.

Return along the narrow path over the flower-bedecked turf to walk to the opposite end of the island. This is the highest point (105 feet) and from here you can see Iona and its abbey.

Fingal's Cave

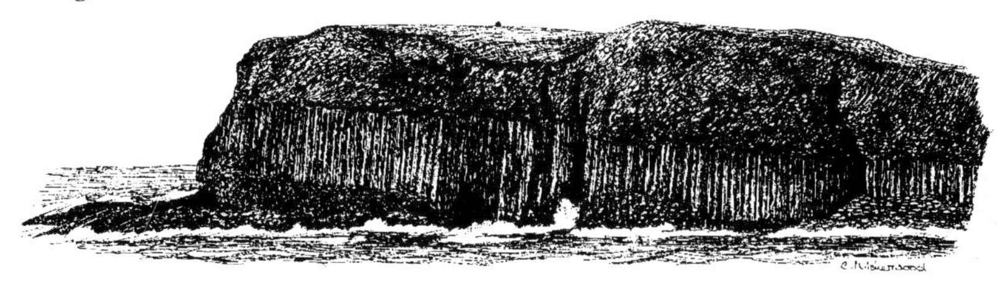